The Student Guide to
OXFORD

A FEW WORDS

This book was written, designed and produced by Publishing students at Oxford Brookes University. However, many other people have been instrumental in bringing this title to print and we would like to take a moment to acknowledge them here.

The inspiration for this guide book came from the students and teachers of Media Studies at the Hogeschool van Amsterdam. A special thanks to Rose Leighton for leading the way for us.

Thank you to the staff at Oxford Brookes University who have shared their knowledge, expertise and enthusiasm; in particular, Helena Markou, Chris Jennings, Adrian Bullock, Sue Miller, Sheila Lambie, and Angus Phillips.

Finally, we would like to acknowledge HEIF for providing the seed funding to bring this book to market.

CONTENTS

Arts & Culture

Sport & Health

Student's Union

Transport

GETTING TO KNOW OXFORD

Oxford: The Facts

Population

General: 151,900 (2011 Census) – Estimated to be 161,000 by 2019

Students: 32,000 studying full-time at the two universities in Oxford

That's 24% of the city's adult population

Multicultural Oxford

Diversity: 28% of Oxford's population were born outside of the UK (2011)

22% of Oxford's population are from an ethnic minority group compared to 13% in the rest of the country

14% of residents are from a white, non-British ethnic background

Ethnic diversity is expected to increase as the percentages are higher in the child population

Economy

4,000 businesses in Oxford, providing 120,000 jobs

Main Oxford industries: Automotive, Education, Healthcare, Hospitality, Publishing, Tourism, and Technology

Around 50% of Oxford's workforce lives outside the city

Tourism
There are 9.5 million visitors per year. This generates £770 million annually for local businesses

Weather Averages
Temperatures: throughout the year average temperatures range between 4°C and 16°C (39°F – 61°F)

Rainfall: 53.08mm per month – around 637mm per year

Daily Sunshine Hours: 3 hours in January to 9 hours in June

Hottest Month: July

Coldest Month: January

Most Rainfall: December

Most Sunshine Hours: June

Oxford Random Trivia

Oxford is steeped in history and culture. Some lesser-known facts are kept hidden away in the depths of the castle dungeons; below are a few of the more interesting and fun ones that could be dug up.

Great Tom, the famous bell in Christ Church Cathedral, strikes 101 times at 21:05 each evening. This dates back to when the college was founded and had 101 students, and it rang to remind each of them that the gates were about to be locked.

In 1556, three men named Cranmer, Latimer and Ridley were burnt at the stake for heresy. A memorial commemorates the event in St Giles; however, the burning took place on what is currently Broad Street.

The John Radcliffe Hospital is world-renowned for its innovative treatments and research. A lesser-known fact is that after Fleming's discovery of penicillin, it was then developed by three Oxford researchers during the early years of the Second World War.

The Headington Shark is one of the most well-known residents of Headington. Bill Heine commissioned it in 1986, and still lives in the house with a headless shark protruding out of his roof. The Council have tried unsuccessfully to have it removed and even offered to re-home it!

Oxford has more published writers per square mile than any other city in the world. Among the most famous have been C. S. Lewis, who wrote *The Chronicles of Narnia*, Lewis Carroll, author of *Alice in Wonderland*, J. R. R. Tolkien who famously wrote *The Hobbit* and *The Lord of the Rings* and P. D. James, who wrote *The Children of Men*.

Oxford is also well known for its famous detective, Morse. Colin Dexter did not reveal his first name, Endeavour, until the 12th novel, keeping TV fans guessing for over three years.

Every visitor to the world-famous Bodleian Library must swear an oath not to light a fire within its walls!

"I am impressed by the history and incredible architecture of Oxford city. The architecture represents English history from the Saxon period to mid 18th Century, and it's no less than heaven for an architecture student like me, as we get lots opportunities to learn from the city itself. The poet Matthew Arnold has rightly described Oxford as a 'city of dreaming spires' in one of his poems."

Aman Kapoor,

Architecture student, from India

A Brief History

The origins of Oxford date back to the Saxon Period. The University of Oxford was founded in the late 12th century; it was to be the first university in England and the oldest in the wider English-speaking world.

Over time tension between the academics and local people grew, and in February 1355, the "town vs. gown" conflicts peaked in the "St Scholastica Day Riot". What started out as a casual pub brawl ended in around 90 deaths of both scholars and townsfolk.

The next event worth knowing took place during the English Civil War, when Oxford temporarily served as the country's capital and King Charles, who had fled from London, held court here from 1642.

Some 260 years later, William Morris started producing his famous small green cars in the city's factories, and Oxford proved itself to be invaluable as an industrial city too.

•TOP 5 OF 5 •

Sights & Places of Interest

University Church of St Mary the Virgin

The largest of Oxford's parish churches. St Mary's tower has 124 steps available for the public to climb and is a prominent feature of the Oxford skyline. The 13th century landmark is situated just off the High Street, where the intricate baroque porch designed by Nicholas Stone meets the street. This beautiful towering architecture cannot be missed. The church is open daily, 9am to 5pm (6am to 6pm in July and August); on Sundays the Tower opens at 12:15pm October to May, 11:15am June to September. Admission for students is £1.50.

Carfax Tower

Largely considered to mark the centre of the city, Carfax Tower is located at the junction between Cornmarket Street, St Aldate's, Queen Street, and the High Street. "Carfax" is derived from the French word meaning "crossroads". The tower is all that remains of the 12th/13th century church that was demolished and moved to the High Street. For spectacular views climb to the top and look across the Oxford skyline. Open daily from April to October, 10am to 5:30pm (4:30pm in October), and November to March, 10am to 3pm (4pm in March). Admission for students is £2.20.

Oxford Castle Quarter

The castle was initially developed back in 1071 for William the Conqueror but was later demolished during the English Civil War. The prison buildings were later restored and Her Majesty's Prison Oxford was established in 1878. In 1996 the prison was officially closed, although guided tours are available around the historic building and visitors can also climb the Norman Castle Mound for a panoramic view of Oxford. The rest of the buildings have been redeveloped as a complex of modern restaurants, as well as the Malmaison Hotel, which is themed on the old prison and is a perfect way to end your visit. | Oxford Castle Quarter, Oxford, OX1 1AY.

Christ Church College

As one of the largest Oxford colleges with the Cathedral Church for the Diocese of Oxford, Christ Church is one of the most visited places in the city. Founded by Cardinal Wolsey in 1525, the buildings were originally named Cardinal College, but in 1546 they were renamed as Christ Church by King Henry VIII. Known for its many famous alumni, as well as being used for film scenes such as The Great Hall in *Harry Potter* films. The Cathedral and Gallery are not to be missed. Open all year round except Christmas Day. | Admission costs £4.50 to £7 depending on which buildings are are open. Last entry is 4:15pm, closing 4:30pm. The Hall is often closed between 11:40am and 2:30pm.

Radcliffe Camera

5

One of the most recognisable buildings in Oxford, the Radcliffe Camera was built in 1737-1749. It was originally built to house the Radcliffe Science Library; 'camera' meaning 'room' in Latin. Designed by James Gibbs, the circular, English Palladian style building creates an iconic landmark. Today, the Camera serves as the main reading room for the University and is open to the public as part of a tour of the Bodleian Library. access through Catte St. | Term time opening hours: Monday to Friday 9am to 10pm, Saturday 10am to 4pm, Sunday 11am to 5pm.

Festivals & Events

Oxford Round Table Firework Display

This annual event is very popular in Oxford. Thousands of people make their way to South Park to watch not only a vast display of fireworks but also a large bonfire, live music, a fun fair, and local food stalls. 2014 marks the 47th annual display and all proceeds from the event go towards local charities in the Oxford area. | South Park, Oxford; 9th November 2014; Gates open at 5pm, Fireworks 6:45pm.

May Morning

For most Oxford residents, May Day marks the coming of spring and is a traditional and festive celebration. The festivities begin at 6am with the choristers of Magdalen College singing the hymn Hymnus Eucharisticus from the Great Tower. Pedestrians can gather on Magdalen Bridge, which will be closed to traffic. However, for students, May Morning signals a marathon pub crawl, as most bars and clubs stay open through the night before.

Cowley Road Carnival

A summer party not to be missed, Cowley Road Carnival celebrates the diverse communities within Oxford with a colourful procession, live bands, and dancers, with venues along the street and a wide selection of food, drink, and other stalls to visit.

Christmas Light Festival

This three-day festival is a city highlight when it comes to starting off the Christmas events. The festival takes place at the end of November, beginning on a Friday with a magical lantern parade, followed by a night of music and dance events on Saturday and a day of song on Sunday. Throughout this long weekend there are late-night and themed openings at the museums and art centres and a Christmas market and fairground in St Giles.

Oxfringe Festival

Oxfringe is an annual festival of literary, theatrical, artistic, and musical events. Officially established in 2007 as two small literary events it has since expanded, attracting thousands of people to over 100 events spread across different venues. Held in early June, the purpose of this event is to promote upcoming artists and provide a chance for the community of Oxford and other audiences to enjoy a wide variety of shows.

Museums

Pitt Rivers & Museum of Natural History

The Pitt Rivers Museum holds an impressive collection centred mainly around anthropology and archaology. It is very different from every other museum you might have visited before. Why? The best way to find out is to visit it yourself! Right next door is the Oxford University Museum of Natural History, known for its Neo-Gothic architecture and its inhabitants, one of which is the famous Dodo. | Parks Road, OX1 3PW; admission is free.

Ashmolean

This amazing building resembles a miniature version of the British Museum in London. The Ashmolean collection embraces cultural artifacts and artworks of all kinds and from all over the world. It is known for its interesting Special Exhibitions and the rooftop Ashmolean Dining Room provides a spectacular view of the heart of the city. | Beaumont St, OX1 2PH; admission is free.

Bodleian Library

The Bodleian is the second-largest library in the world, holding over 11 million items. Tours will lead you in and around the magnificent architecture that the famous scar-faced wizard sneaked around in. There are also exhibitions on rare and special books, which are usually accompanied by a number of events. | Broad Street, OX1 3BG Oxford; admission for exhibition free, tours £7 (no concessions).

History of Science Museum

In the History of Science Museum you can marvel at a unique collection of historical scientific instruments. The museum also offers a range of special exhibitions and workshops in collaboration with leading experts in the history of science. Who would have thought that science could be so beautiful? | Broad St, Oxford OX1 3AZ; admission is free.

Museum of Oxford

The Museum of Oxford is dedicated to the history of the city and its inhabitants. Visitors can listen to stories about local people such as Alice Liddell and William Morris and discover local artists. | St Aldate's, OX1 1BX Oxford; admission is free.

Remember public museums
and galleries in the UK are free.
So go and explore!

Galleries

Christ Church Picture Gallery

Should you ever feel like seeing some "proper art", then visit Christ Church Picture Gallery. Its famous drawing collection includes works by Michelangelo, Raphael, and Dürer, and it is definitely worth paying the Old Masters a visit. | Enter through Canterbury Gate at Oriel Square; admission £3.20, students free.

Modern Art Oxford

This gallery is dedicated to modern and contemporary art. It has gained an international reputation for its exhibitions and its role in art education. Apart from exhibitions, it also hosts a range of interesting evening events, such as talks and contemporary music and film nights. | 30 Pembroke Street, Oxford OX1 1BP; admission to the gallery is free.

O3 Gallery

Set in a former prison, the circular room of the O3 gives further space to contemporary arts in Oxford. It also provides a great venue for arts and crafts networking and the local art community. | Oxford Castle, New Rd, Oxford OX1 1AY; admission free

Old Fire Station

4 The Old Fire Station is a gallery in the widest sense. It is devoted to modern and contemporary arts, but is unique due to a great number of events taking place there every month, ranging from dance, music and drama to vintage fairs. | 40 George St, Oxford OX1 2AQ; admission to the exhibitions varies.

Oxford Explore

5 This is a portable gallery: as many parts of Oxford look like the insides of a museum, the city of dreaming spires is a great piece of art in itself. The Oxford Explore Portable Gallery is an app that will allow you to make the most of your city walks, supporting it with vintage views, film material, and stories about the historical city.

Outside Oxford

Although there are hundreds of iconic things to see in Oxford, if you crave travel and new experiences then here's a few ideas of attractions outside Oxford.

Woodstock

Woodstock is 8 miles away but seems like a different world. The quaint village boasts the Oxford Museum and old-fashioned tearooms, coffee shops, and pubs. If you're looking for something a bit grander then look no further than the birthplace of Winston Churchill, Blenheim Palace. Set in 2,000 acres of beautiful parkland, walking around is a day out in itself, but the house is open to visitors too. To end your day you could take a stroll round to St Martin's Church in Bladon, and visit Churchill's grave; it's about half an hour's walk away.

Henley

The town of Henley, in South Oxfordshire, dates back to the 12th Century. It is more of a trek at 24 miles away, but worth the visit. It is most famous for the Henley Regatta, first held 1839, and now annually in June; the atmosphere encompasses the whole town. You can watch the boat races or visit pop-up bars, restaurants, and shops. Henley also offers boat trips down the Thames, and tours of the River and Rowing Museum. Just three miles out of Henley is Greys Court: a beautiful sixteenth-century mansion and gardens. This is a must-see if you are visiting Henley.

Chipping Norton

Chipping Norton is at the gateway to the Cotswolds and is a highly popular tourist town. It is worth spending the whole day wandering around and taking in the scenery. There is a vast array of antique, ceramic, and glass shops, and Wednesday is market day! If you're looking for a bit of culture then the theatre hosts a variety of shows from the contemporary to classics.

Stratford-upon-Avon

Stratford-upon-Avon is an essential visit. The birthplace of Shakespeare offers a multitude of things to do. You can take in a play at the Royal Shakespeare Theatre or do a brass rubbing at the local centre; but if you would like a more weird yet wonderful place to visit then try MAD, the museum of Mechanical Art and Design. Later on in the day, ghost walks take place in the city with tales of local witches, murders, and mysteries.

Milton Keynes

Milton Keynes is a big contrast to the other four must-visit places. It was founded in 1987 and is famous for being home to over 200 roundabouts! If it's adventure and adrenaline you are looking for then this is for you. As well as home to the MK shopping centre with over 200 stores and an open market, the city boasts Xscape. Here you can go to the snow-dome, do some rock climbing, or for something a bit less risky there is the cinema and bowling alley!

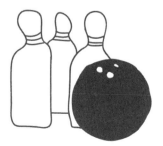

"I really like Oxford because it's not too big, it's not too small, it's close to London, and it has everything you need. Plus it is a beautiful city with a lot of history and many different things to do and see."

Natalia Cabezuelo Martos,

Law student, from Spain

LIVING & WORKING

Oxford is one of the best cities in the world to live in (but we would say that!). It is big enough to have the infrastructure and facilities you expect from a modern European city, but small enough to retain a sense of local community. People are drawn here from all corners of the globe and it is this multi-cultural identity that infuses so much vibrancy into Oxford's culture, music, food and industry.

Finding Accommodation

With two universities and four hospitals within a two mile radius of Oxford's city centre there is no shortage of demand for rented accommodation. Freshers get priority placements in the Brookes student halls and Oxford Colleges, and both have services to help new and returning students find a place to live. These websites contain useful information for anyone planning to live and study in Oxford.

> University of Oxford Accommodation
> www.admin.ox.ac.uk/accommodation/
>
> Oxford Brookes Accommodation Bureau
> www.brookes.ac.uk/studying-at-brookes/
> accommodation/

For the self-sufficient readers, here are our top tips and tactics on finding somewhere to call "home".

100% student house: If you are a full-time student (over 21 hours per week) living with other full-time students on a course lasting at least one year, then you can apply for exemption from paying UK council tax. Council tax ranges from £1,000-£3,500 per year, so you want to avoid this bill if possible.
www.gov.uk/council-tax/full-time-students

Early birds: If you like to get ahead of the crowd, January is the earliest you should start looking for somewhere to live in September! Before Christmas is pushing it (even for the uber-organised).

Just-in-time project managers: If you want to catch houses as they come on to the market, set aside eight weeks before your move-in date as this is often when properties begin to be advertised. Plan for an intensive fortnight of house searching if this is your strategy.

Leave it late: If you can hold off till the end of October, after the September rush has passed, then you may be able to negotiate a better deal with a panicked landlord who hasn't managed to find tenants. You'll need nerves of steel with this strategy, as sometimes the student houses that are left unoccupied aren't the cleanest of properties.

Estate agents: **Love them or hate them, they'll always put the interests of their clients (the homeowner) first. So make sure you get your tenancy agreement and inventory checked by someone with a keen eye for detail.**

Know your tenancy rights: **UK law states that your estate agent or landlord should place any deposit you give them in a protected account. This is called a Tenancy Protection Deposit, and they should provide you with a receipt to prove this has been done. This website has all the details:** www.gov.uk/tenancy-deposit-protection

Daily Info

For over 50 years, the *Daily Info* news bulletin has been brightening up public walls around the city. Each week, on Tuesdays and Fridays, A2 posters are published and displayed around Oxford. The website has the most up-to-date listings. If you want to find a private landlord (and avoid visiting an estate agent), *Daily Info* is one of the best places to look. Or if you have found a house but need a roommate you can place a "no frills" advert on the website for free. www.dailyinfo.co.uk

Other similar sites are www.gumtree.com/oxford **and** www.accommodationforstudents.com

Common Sense Alert!

Be careful with your personal information when placing ads online. Don't include your phone number or email address unnecessarily.

Don't hand over a cash deposit to a private landlord under duress. If they are a reputable landlord they won't mind waiting for you to check that the tenancy agreement is in order.

Do your homework: seek out trustworthy advice from your university or college before entering into a tenancy agreement with an unknown landlord or estate agent. The Students' Union is a good place to find more information.

Removals & Storage

Those coming to Oxford as an undergraduate may move to different accommodation each year. If you don't have a car, and can't fit all your stuff in a taxi, don't worry: just call the Oxford Van Man 01865 362424,
www.oxfordvanman.co.uk. He charges by the hour though, so have everything packed and ready to go before he arrives.

If you have a gap between your tenancies then there are a number of self-storage services situated around the edges of the city. A small locker (1m x 1m x 1m) can cost as little as £5 per week, which is a lot cheaper than extending your rent over the holidays. Here are just a few:

- Big Yellow Self Storage
- Fort Box
- Magenta
- Storage King

Buying the Essentials

Stationery Suppliers **Ryman and WHSmith are the two
shops in Oxford city centre that will cater for all your
needs when it comes to stationery. Whether you need
notepads, pens or Post-it notes, you will find everything
here. Ryman is located on Queen Street and WHSmith is
located on Cornmarket. Staples is also a great place to find
all office supplies, situated on Park End Street.**

Home and kitchenware **If you're looking for a one-stop
shop, head over to Argos! Argos stocks over 33,000
products including kitchen appliances such as toasters,
kettles, rice cookers and microwaves. You can also buy
lamps, desk chairs, bedding and room decorations here.
To buy in Argos, you need to use the catalogues supplied
in-store and note down reservation numbers of the items
you want to purchase. You then take this to the till to pay,
and you will receive the items you would like. There are
two stores in Oxford, one in the city centre, the second on
Botley Road.**

**Just round the corner from the Argos in the city centre
is Robert Dyas, crammed full of kitchen and household
essentials.**

There are a number of independent homestores in Headington and on Cowley Road, which you will recognise by the curious arrangement of plastic boxes, mops, plant pots and other random items in front of the shop window. They stock a hilarious range of miscellaneous "stuff" that you think you'll never need... until you do.

Working & Internships

If you are lucky you may be able to find something that matches your area of study, but if not don't worry. All work experience will look good on your CV, provide transferable skills, and give you an opportunity to build a professional network. You never know who might be able to help you with a reference or a job in the future. Here are some things you should know:

Our first piece of advice would be to settle in and get a feel for your academic workload before committing yourself to a part-time job. Working till 3am in a bar might earn you some spending money, but oversleeping and missing lectures as a result will cost you more in wasted tuition fees.

Check how many hours you are allowed to work per week according to your Visa Restrictions and be careful not to exceed the legal limit.

Companies offering internships should at the very least cover your travel expenses. An internship might involve job shadowing, ad hoc tasks or mini-projects. However, if you are being asked to do the equivalent work of a full-time member of staff, over a prolonged period of time, then you should be paid the minimum wage.

We have a minimum wage in the UK. It is currently £6.50 for anyone over the age of 21, £5.13 for 18-20 yr olds and £3.79 for under 18s.

Money Saving Tips

Buy in bulk Easier if you are living in a shared house as opposed to halls. Buying the valuable student commodities in bulk saves money and hassle e.g. pasta, milk, shampoo, eggs, toilet paper, in fact anything that won't go off in a hurry! Plus, multipacks of anything that are on offer at the supermarkets.

Shop online For food or clothes especially, buying online is a wonderful timesaver (so long as you don't get sucked into the black hole of the internet) and it can save you serious cash. Grocery shopping online means no impulse purchases of shiny things that catch your eye and no pricey bus fares to the out-of-town supermarket. Clothes shopping online often means special discounts, and most sites have a 'shopping basket' that tots up your spend as you add more clothes to it, so you don't get a nasty shock at the till.

Get all the cards except for those nasty store cards! Being a student means you are eligible for lots of discount cards. For example, a National Railcard gives you a third off every train journey you make. NUS cards save you money at clothes shops, restaurants, and pretty much everywhere you can think of.

Buy a printer this sounds expensive, but it really isn't. You don't need to spend a fortune on a new shiny printer with all the gadgets. Instead, try websites like Gumtree or Preloved, where you can pick up a good quality printer for a fraction of the new price – and if you pick it up in person, you can ask the seller to demonstrate the printer is working. University printers are sometimes broken or jammed, and by the time you reach the front of the queue for the one working printer (which half the campus is using), you're charged a fortune per sheet. Printing at home is simpler and a lot, lot cheaper.

Don't buy snacks from the campus shops Lectures invariably make students crave crisps, chocolate, water, fizzy drinks, and come the mid-lecture break, it is tempting to pop into the campus shop and grab handfuls of sugary goodies to keep you going 'til later. But if you buy your crisps or chocolate bars in multipack from your local pound shop or supermarket, it is a lot cheaper than buying everything individually. Water bottles can be reused by filling them up from your hall's tap, or a water fountain on campus. You can even bring in your own thermos of tea or coffee, and feel suitably smug as others fuss over burnt fingers and flimsy cardboard cups.

Work that chunky knit like it's 1989 For people living in student houses rather than all-inclusive halls, heating can absolutely burn money. When the dry, bone-cold Oxford winter hits, don't be tempted to whack up the heating – instead, layer up! Invest in a 15-tog duvet, be sure to shut windows (and curtains in the evening), and don't walk around the house in skimpy clothes and goosebumps. You don't have to totally stop using the heating – just use it sparingly.

Watch your water use **If you're in all-inclusive halls, now is your chance to go wild with your water usage, because you'll be worrying about it in later years. When you are out of halls and paying separately for water, little things like leaving the taps running when you brush your teeth, or spending hours beautifying yourself in the shower will come back to haunt you when the water bill comes in. Not to mention, no house-sharer likes a shower hog.**

"Sometimes studying abroad can be lonely. In Oxford, I feel confident because I'm not alone; there are lots of international students from all over the world here."

Yurika Sugita,

International Relations student, from Japan

EATING & DRINKING

If you fancy a bite to eat out in the city of Oxford, then the possibilities are endless! It is filled with a variety of restaurants, bistros, cafeterias, diners, bars, and pubs – all suiting different wants and needs!

A Taste of Home

Living in a new place can be a bit of a culture shock for international students, especially if you are not familiar with European food. But large supermarkets like Sainsbury's and Tesco on the ring road have "World Food" sections, stocking popular staples from Indian, Asian, Caribbean, and Eastern European cuisines. Oxford also has a number of specialist food shops (predominantly along the Cowley Road) where you can buy groceries from around the world, often at a lower price than at the big supermarkets. Here are just a few of them.

"日本食コーナー"

For Chinese, Thai, Japanese and Korean supplies
Thong Heng, 6 Windmill Road, Headington, OX3 7BX
Lung Wah Chong, 41-42 Hythe Bridge Street, OX1 2EP
Jing Jing Oriental Food Store, 188 Cowley Road, OX4 1UE

"طعم الوطن"

For Polish supplies
Polish Food, 168 Cowley Road, Oxford, OX4 1UE
Polish Food, 34 Cowley Road, Littlemore, OX4 4LD
Euro Foods, 115 London Road, Headington, OX3 9HZ

"Smak kuchni domowej"

"Μια γεύση πατρίδα"

For Mediterranean supplies
Meli Deli (Greek), 51a Cowley Road, Oxford, OX4 1HP
Il Principe Italian Deli, 82 Cowley Road, Oxford, OX4 1JB

For Caribbean supplies
Da Root, 2-4 Windmill Rd, Oxford, OX3 7BX

For Eastern, Middle Eastern, and halal supplies
Maroc Deli, 66 Cowley Road, Oxford, OX4 1JB
Simply Fresh, 236-238 Cowley Road, Oxford, OX4 1UH
Tahmid Stores, 53 Cowley Road, Oxford, OX4 1HP

"यहाँ ऑक्सफोर्ड में आपको भारत की तरह शाकाहारी भोजन मिल सकता है"

A Taste of Britain

Eating out can be expensive, and not always an option on a student budget. But for those who want to try typically British food without spending a fortune we have picked out some of the nation's favourite foods.

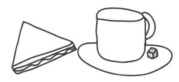

Fish and chips Deep-fried fish in a tempura style batter with a generous side portion of deep-fried potato chips. Traditionally seasoned with salt and malt vinegar. This can be accompanied by gravy, curry sauce, mushy peas or pickled onions (depending on which part of the UK you come from).

You can find this in takeaway outlets around Oxford, and it costs around £6. Dish size varies, but often one portion of fish and chips will feed two people.

The late-night kebab Grilled lamb meat in spices. Comes in two varieties, the Doner Kebab, where the meat is ground up with spices and grilled on a rotisserie, and the Shish Kebab where cut pieces of whole meat are marinated in spices and grilled on skewers. Traditionally eaten in a pitta bread. This can be accompanied with chips, salad, mayonnaise or chilli sauce.

You can find these in the evening to early morning, sold from vans (with kitchens inside them) and cost £3-5. They usually park along the High Street, St Aldate's, St Giles in the city centre and by the shops in Headington. Kebab Kid and Bodrum on the Cowley Road offer halal kebabs.

Cheese on toast with Worcestershire Sauce (pronounced woo-ster). A very affordable classic snack to try at home. You will need:

*   cheddar cheese,
*   sliced white bread,
*   bottle of Worcestershire Sauce (stocked by most supermarkets – usually on a shelf near the tomato ketchup).

Start by lightly toasting one side of your bread under a grill. Turn the bread over and cover in sliced or grated cheese, sprinkle with Worcestershire Sauce, grill until the cheese has fully melted and begins to bubble. And there you have it - steaming hot cheese on toast!

Fancy cream tea A pot of tea served with a selection of savoury sandwiches, sweet scones (with jam and cream) and cake. Traditionally cream tea is eaten in the mid-afternoon to keep you going till dinner time. However, it is no small snack, so make sure you arrive hungry. Costing between £10-20, this might be one to reserve for special occasions, or a treat when your parents come to town.

You can find cream teas in hotels and restaurants around town; we recommend The Grand Café, the Randolph Hotel, and The Vaults & Garden Café in the city centre.

The mighty Sunday roast Nothing better to warm you up on a chilly winter's day than a plate of oven-roasted food in a warm, cosy pub. The star of the show is roast Beef, Lamb, Chicken, or Pork joint. This comes served with a selection of roast potatoes, vegetables, Yorkshire pudding, stuffing, gravy and condiments. Guaranteed to fill you up!

Available from almost every Oxford pub on Sundays (and sometimes throughout the week too), prices can vary from £8-12. We recommend the Angel & Greyhound, The Britannia Inn, O'Neills, the Turf Tavern and The Royal Oak.

City Centre

The city centre is a great place to start if you're looking for a place to drink and dine in a central location. George street is lined with restaurants and pubs: for upmarket dining, visit Jamie's Italian, a restaurant owned by celebrity chef Jamie Oliver. Although slightly pricier, it is still affordable so could be a great place to impress a date without breaking the bank, and it has deliciously fresh and filling food.

Alternatively, there are many other Italian restaurants located on George Street such as Bella Italia and Zizzi Ristorante, which offer similarly priced food.

Oxford is home to many restaurants offering the Wetherspoon's menu – perfect for students on a budget. There are two located in the city centre: Four Candles is on George Street, surrounded by burger restaurants such as the Gourmet Burger Kitchen, the Wig and Pen and Byron Hamburgers; The Swan & Castle is on Castle Street.

Oxford does exceedingly well with its pubs, most of which offer quality home-cooked food. One of the most popular as well as historic pubs is the Turf Tavern. Tucked down a small alley and dating back to the 13th Century, the Turf Tavern appears to be the perfect haven for a weary tourist, or fatigued students. On entering the small green front door, you are greeted by a strong aroma of well rested British beers. It usually has 10 guest ales plus a range of spirits, ciders, and soft drinks. It comes as a great surprise to hear the Turf Tavern offer taster glasses, just to make sure you have made the correct choice. The food menu offers homely, well-cooked food, boasting about its quality fish and chips. After ordering both food and drink at the bar, there is a wide choice of seats in and around the pub, with each area of the garden representing a great atmosphere and mix of guests visiting the famous pub.

Oxford's Covered Market offers numerous independent cafés such as Brown's Café, Ricardo's, Alpha Bar, Oxford Café, and the Pieminister. All of them sell wholesome and fresh food at affordable prices, so pop inside for a light lunch.

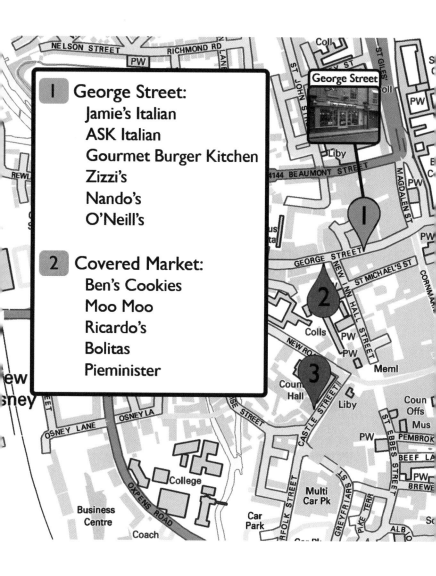

1 George Street:
- Jamie's Italian
- ASK Italian
- Gourmet Burger Kitchen
- Zizzi's
- Nando's
- O'Neill's

2 Covered Market:
- Ben's Cookies
- Moo Moo
- Ricardo's
- Bolitas
- Pieminister

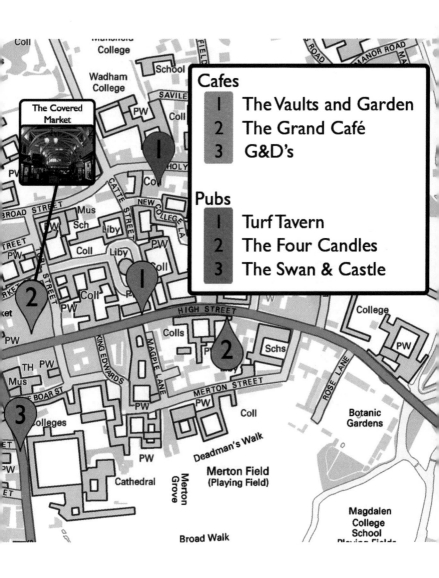

Cafes

1 The Vaults and Garden
2 The Grand Café
3 G&D's

Pubs

1 Turf Tavern
2 The Four Candles
3 The Swan & Castle

Cowley Road

A multicultural hotbed of cafés and shops, Cowley Road is a great place to visit for someone with a wide flavour palette. The Mirch Masala is a delightfully friendly Indian Restaurant whose menu holds a wide range of different curries and other dishes, which can all be tailored to your spice tolerance. However, Cowley Road also has a host of Indian eateries such as Akash, Al Mumbai and Aziz.

There is a variety of multicultural cuisine available, including Chinese restaurants and takeaways such as Chopsticks, and the Rice Box. For a Mediterranean dish visit Café Baba which offers delicious tapas..

Verde Pizzeria is a family-run Italian restaurant situated on Cowley Road. With locally-sourced food used in recipes that have been passed down generations, Verde offers a range of pasta, pizza, fish, meat, and vegetarian dishes.

Cowley Road is also home to a variety of cafés. One of the most popular is the indie music shop the Truck Store that has its own café inside called The Keen Bean. It has a warm and friendly vibe, with indie music playing softly in the background. It is a brilliant place to sit and enjoy a hot coffee.

Refresh Café is a great place to go for that well-needed hangover breakfast A large fry-up accompanied by a tea or coffee will make you feel better for merely a fiver, and they're not leaving anything out: bacon, eggs, sausages, mushrooms, tomatoes, beans, black pudding, and toast will all fill your stomach. The best part is, if there's something you don't like you can swap it for extra of what you do like! The volunteer staff are all incredibly friendly.

To all sweet-toothed students, behold G&D's. Established in 1992 by George Stroup and Davis Roberts, G&D's has over the years become the late-night, mid-day and even early-morning place to get your daily sugar fix. Offering a wide range of handmade ice cream combinations, G&D boasts three branches: George and Davis in Little Clarendon Street; George and Danver on St Aldate's; and George and Delila on Cowley Road. Students can meet from 8am till midnight every day of the week.

All three branches offer a light, friendly and comfortable setting, perfect for a quiet night out with some friends. Ice cream wise, it is all handmade on location, with the ingredients sourced fresh and locally around the Oxford area. Some flavour options include: 'After Eight Mint', 'White Gold' (white chocolate, butterscotch and cookie dough), 'Bananarama' (banana), 'Oxford Blue' (blueberry), 'Smelly Bee' (lavender & honey) and 'Hamlet' (white chocolate and raspberry).

If you thought everything mentioned above couldn't get better, G&D's also provide savoury bagels as well as a wide selection of freshly baked goods for you to choose from.

Cowley Road is also a great place to start if you have certain dietary requirements.

Atomic Burger and Atomic Pizza allow customers to personalise every aspect of their meal, making it easy for veggies and vegans, and they also make fresh gluten-free burgers, buns and pizza bases. They can be found on opposite ends of Cowley Road.

Red Star is the place to go If you're in the mood for noodles. The staff are extremely knowledgeable about the ingredients used and can use gluten-free soy sauce upon request

Tick Tock Café If you are wanting a full English after a night out then head over to the Tick Tock Café, who offer vegetarian breakfasts and gluten-free sausages.

We can't forget the horde of pubs and bars lining the streets. Right at the beginning of Cowley Road is the popular City Arms, which boasts a wide range of events to ensure you'll never have a dull night. With £1-a-pint nights, live music and pub quizzes, it is a pub that can easily be described as having a student atmosphere. If you're a sports fan then the HD and 3D plasma TVs that host live sport will probably be of interest to you – as well as the pool table, football table and air hockey located in the heart of the pub.

The Cowley Retreat is at the heart of Cowley Road, offering a fantastic range of draught beers and ales, wines and in-house cocktails. It is ideal for a friendly drink with friends or for a weekend warm-up.

The Library. Don't let the name fool you - it is no quiet study area but a delightfully student-friendly pub which offers a range of well-priced drinks, including slushies!

Bar Aroma is a well-established bar which has knowledgeable and experienced staff who can make you any cocktail to suit your fancy at student-friendly prices! Open from 6pm until 2am except on a Friday and Saturday, when it opens an hour earlier at 5pm.

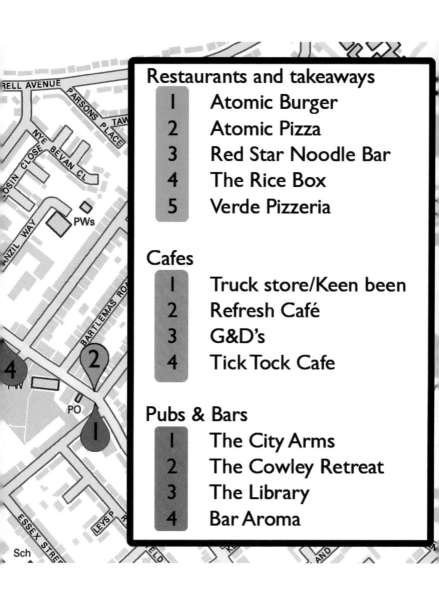

Restaurants and takeaways

1   Atomic Burger
2   Atomic Pizza
3   Red Star Noodle Bar
4   The Rice Box
5   Verde Pizzeria

Cafes

1   Truck store/Keen been
2   Refresh Café
3   G&D's
4   Tick Tock Cafe

Pubs & Bars

1   The City Arms
2   The Cowley Retreat
3   The Library
4   Bar Aroma

St Clement's

Close to Cowley Road, St Clement's is home to many restaurants and pubs.

The Pink Giraffe is a Chinese restaurant with one of the best menus around for vegetarians - not to mention the food is outstanding.

La Cucina is an Italian restaurant close by, for people who want to embrace the real Italian experience. It is also good if you have special dietary requirements as it serves gluten-free pasta.

St Clement's is more known for its range of pubs. These include The Port Mahon, which offers home-cooked food and a lively atmosphere where everyone gathers to watch Sky Sports and live music. They also put on a quiz night on Sundays from 8pm, so go along and wow everybody with your knowledge! Other pub restaurants include Moya, Angel & Greyhound and The Old Black Horse.

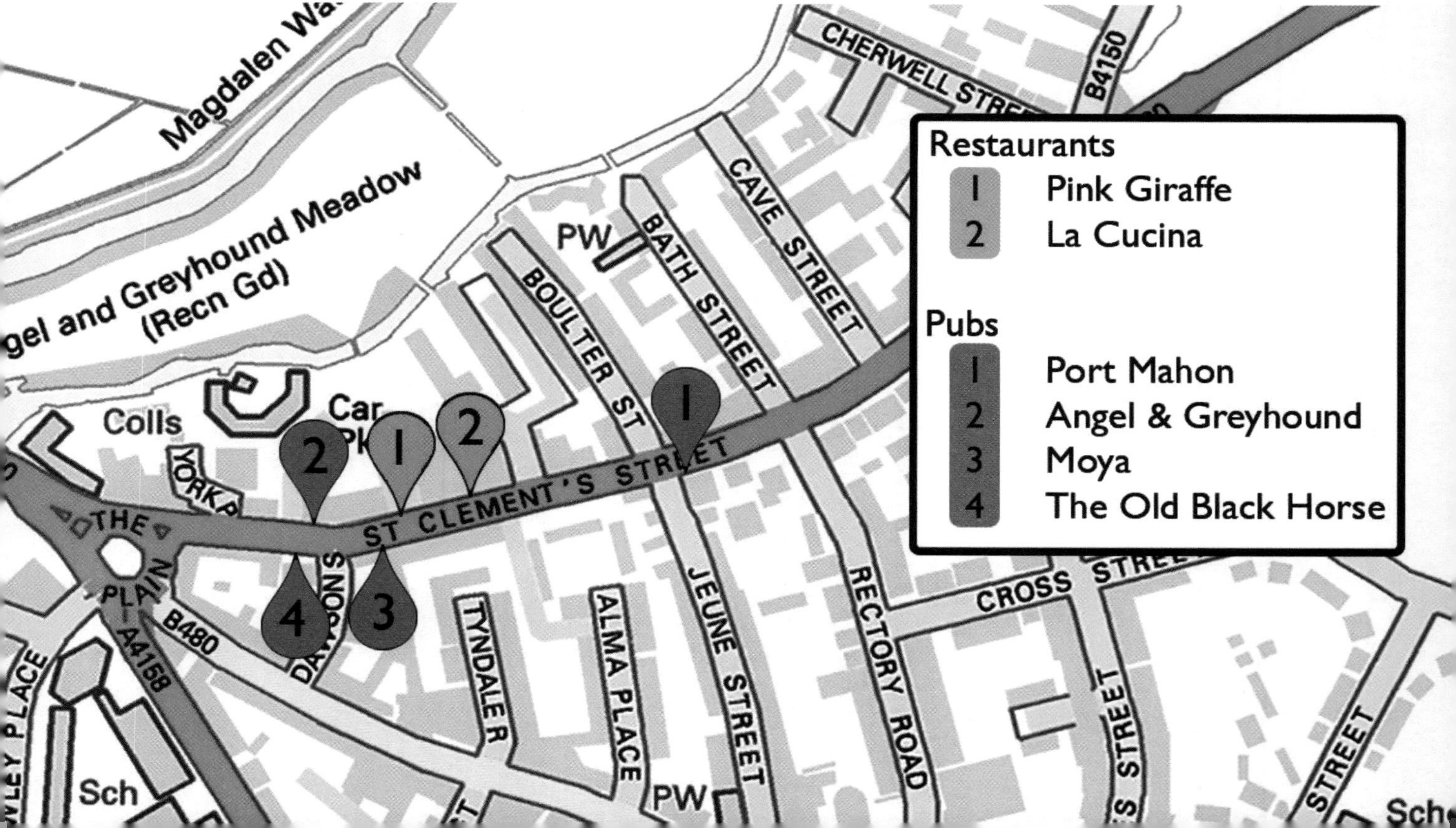

Restaurants
1 Pink Giraffe
2 La Cucina
Pubs
1 Port Mahon
2 Angel & Greyhound
3 Moya
4 The Old Black Horse
Magdalen Wa
gel and Greyhound Meadow
(Recn Gd)
CHERWELL STRE
B4150
CAVE STREET
BATH STREET
BOULTER ST
PW
ST CLEMENT'S STREET
Car Pk
Colls
YORK P
THE PLAIN
B480
A4158
DAWSONS
TYNDALE R
ALMA PLACE
JEUNE STREET
RECTORY ROAD
CROSS STREET
STREET
Sch

"I love the Oxford music scene! Every night of the week there is a variety of gigs happening in pubs and clubs around the city. The tricky bit is deciding which one to go to."

Helena Markou,

Vocalist for Tiger Mendoza, from Oxford

ARTS & CULTURE

Oxford boasts most of the high street and designer shops that we know and love in the UK but, unusually, it also has a host of individual shops that you will only find here! Along with these there are a range of markets that take place either weekly or monthly. Oxford Fashion Week is also held in venues around the city so don't worry if you can't make it to London or Paris – we have our very own! For those interested in entertainment, there is plenty of choice here in Oxford, ranging from cinemas and theatres to music venues and events.

Shopping

Oxford City Centre Oxford's main shopping area is within the city centre – easy to access by both bus and train, but slightly more difficult by car due to the one way system. There is a large variety of shops across various streets including: High Street, Turl Street, Queen Street, St Aldate's, Cornmarket, and Broad Street. As the centre of Oxford is pretty small, these streets are very close together, making it easy for you to navigate around the shops. The shopping area is surrounded by many of Oxford University's prestigious colleges, making for a beautiful setting in which to spend your money. Thursday is the city centre's late night shopping day when most shops will be open past the usual 6pm closing time. In the city centre there are two small shopping centres; Westgate and Clarendon.

Westgate Shopping Centre Located near Bonn Square on Queen Street. Shops here include: Primark, Sports Direct, Thornton's Chocolate, Claire's Accessories, and Whittards of Chelsea. It also has a customer car park accessible from Norfolk Street.

Opening hours:
Monday to Wednesday: 9am to 5:30pm.
Thursday: 9am to 8pm.
Friday to Saturday: 9am to 5:30pm.
Sunday: 11am to 5pm.
www.westgateoxford.co.uk

Clarendon Shopping Centre The Clarendon Shopping Centre can be accessed from Cornmarket Street and Queen Street. Shops here include: Zara, Ansari, Costa Coffee, French Connection, and GAP. There is no adjacent car park, however it is easily accessible by bus and is located near the Westgate Shopping Centre.

Templars Square, Cowley Templars Square is based in Cowley and has two affordable car parks nearby. One car park can be accessed from Cromwell Road, the second accessed from Hockmore Street. Both car parks are open Monday to Saturday from 7am until 6:30pm and Sunday from 9:30am to 4:30pm. Shops here include: Dorothy Perkins, Toy Galaxy, Boots, and New Look.
www.templarssquare.com

Opening hours:
Monday to Wednesday: 8am to 6pm.
Thursday: 8am to 7pm.
Friday to Saturday: 8am to 6pm.
Sunday: 10:30am to 5pm.
www.clarendoncentre.co.uk

Fashion

Vintage Fairs Oxford is a great place for vintage fairs, hosting many each year. The most famous vintage fair is Lou Lou's Vintage Fair, which takes place four times a year in Oxford Town Hall. It has more than 50 stalls of vintage fashion, accessories, homeware and jewellery for both men and women. There is also a vintage beauty parlour where you can get your hair and makeup done in true vintage style. The café provides a range of refreshments and cream teas. On their Facebook page you can find more information about dates, times, and how to get involved: www.facebook.com/oxfordvintage.

Oxford Fashion Week Oxford Fashion Week is one of the UK's leading fashion weeks; it is an annual independent fashion showcase lasting for one week only in venues around Oxford. Founded in 2009, it has showcased designers such as Alexander McQueen and Matthew Williamson as well as a wide variety of up-and-coming talents.

This event is mostly produced by volunteers from across the UK and it takes place in a range of venues across the city such as the Sheldonian Theatre, the Ashmolean Museum, Oxford Town Hall and many others.

The shows are arranged by clothing category, and usually consist of, among others, a concept fashion show, a ready-to-wear show and a *haute couture* show. The catwalk shows feature a mix of well-known professional models as well as new faces that often get discovered right here in Oxford.

Each year the week varies but you can discover everything you need to know about the time, place and how to get tickets through their website:
www.oxfordfashionweek.co.uk.

Markets

Covered Market Oxford's Covered Market has been trading for over 200 years and is home to a range of shops: luxury foods, cookies and cake shops, cafés, clothes shops, and much more. If you are looking for a slice of Oxford to keep with you forever you will almost certainly find it in the Covered Market. There are plenty of shops where you can buy gifts and keepsakes to remember your time here. Not only is the Covered Market perfect for gifts, fashion and yummy cakes and sweets; it also holds a butcher, fishmonger and a fresh fruit and vegetable stall. The Covered Market can be accessed from the High Street, Market Street, or through Golden Cross in Cornmarket.

> ### Opening hours
> Monday to Saturday from 9am to 5:30pm
> Sunday from 10am to 4pm
> www.oxford-coveredmarket.co.uk/
>
> Note: check the website for specific days as some stalls are not open on Sundays

Gloucester Green Gloucester Green holds various markets throughout the week. The Gloucester Green Market is held every Wednesday and Thursday from 9am to 4pm. This market sells general produce from fruit and vegetables to sweets and confectionery, as well as fabrics and crafts. This market is perfect if you are looking to do your grocery shopping as the produce is fresh and very reasonably priced. It is run by the Oxford City Council.

Gloucester Green Farmers Market. The market is held on the first and third Thursday of every month, from 9am to 3pm. Much like the Gloucester Green Market, it is perfect for fruit and vegetables, especially if you are looking to try some of the local produce that has been grown around Oxfordshire.

www.skettsfarmersmarkets.co.uk/

Gloucester Green Antiques and Craft Market If you are looking for an antique gem or like to try crafts, this is the place for you. This market was established in 1990 and is held every Thursday from 9am to 4pm. Here you can find yourself an antique bargain for your university room or maybe even to take home as a gift. You'll find all types of antique gems from furniture to jewellery. If craft is more your thing then you'll have fun finding some craft materials. There is also clothes shopping to be done; whether you're looking for vintage, retro or new.

www.lsdpromotions.com/oxford/

Craft & Fabric Shops

Darn It & Stitch A bijou haberdashery situated in the town centre on Blue Boar Street. They stock a small but quirky range of wools, yarns, fabrics and accessories. www.darnitandstitch.com,

Oxford Yarn Store Located slightly off the beaten track in North Parade they stock a wide range of colourful yarns for knitting and crocheting. www.oxfordyarnstore.co.uk

Each of these independent retailers host regular crafting events from knitting to spinning and lacemaking. It is well worth visiting their websites or popping in to find out about the range of workshops they offer.

Cinemas

"Want to catch a film? If you're looking to have a night out at the cinema instead of a wild night at Fuzzies or Park End then there is a choice of cinemas in Oxford conveniently dotted around the city."

Odeon One of the more popular cinemas is the Odeon Cinema on George Street. Not only is it in the centre of Oxford, it is also near several great restaurants. Why not make it a night out with your friends? Another benefit is that this cinema has a taxi rank right outside the door. George Street, OX1 2BL | www.odeon.co.uk

Based just around the corner, Odeon Magdalen Street is a little smaller but widens your chances of getting a ticket! It is just as convenient for transport and restaurants. Magdalen Street, OX1 3AE

Vue If you have a car you can always travel to the Vue Cinema, a 20-minute ride away from Oxford City centre. It's situated in the Ozone Leisure Park which also offers other entertainment activities, such as bowling. You can also get there via public transport. Grenoble Road OX4 4XP | Tel: 08712240240 | www.myvue.com

Is it worth it? It may be slightly further away but Vue has Sony 4K Digital screens with higher quality Dolby 'Profound Sound!'

The Phoenix Picturehouse

As part of the Picturehouse chain, the Phoenix Picturehouse is found in Oxford and not only shows new and upcoming movies but also holds events. This cinema has a bar on the first floor, allowing you to chill and discuss the movie; it can also be hired out for private events. The Phoenix Picturehouse also hosts E4 Slackers Club, where once a month, usually on a Thursday, the cinema shows free student previews exclusively to Slackers members. To become a member, you just need to take your NUS or student card into the Picturehouse and join for free! 57 Walton Street, Oxford, OX2 6AE | Tel: 08719025736 | www.picturehouses.co.uk

The Ultimate Picture Palace

The Ultimate Picture Palace is the oldest independent cinema in Oxford. There is only one screen, but don't let that put you off; they not only show newly released blockbusters but also foreign, indie and classic films, as well as documentaries. With a bar for snacks and drinks, this cosy cinema is perfect for a great night out. Very few adverts are shown before the film begins so it is best to be on time to catch your movie! The cinema is close to St Clement's Street and is just along Cowley Road. It can also be hired out for private screenings and meetings. Jeune Street, Cowley Road OX4 1XP | Tel: 01865245288 | http://www.uppcinema.com

Music

Oxford is packed with many great places to go if you are in the mood for music, and there is always likely to be something on within your favourite genre. A good thing about Oxford is that the prices for events reflect the fact that the city population is dominated by students.

Nightshift Magazine

This free music magazine is published once a month and contains all the music listings for events around the city. It also contains reviews of events and music released by Oxford bands. If you are looking for a night out with live music you can pick up a free copy from shops, pubs and venues or download from http://nightshift.oxfordmusic.net/

other useful links:
www.musicinoxford.co.uk/events
www.oxfordplayhouse.com/ticketsoxford
www.inoxford.com/music/music_details

Festivals & Events

There is a wide range of music festivals in and around Oxford throughout the year, but July and August are the busiest months. We've picked out some of our favourites for you!

January to March

Oxford Music Festival: Local classical musicians perform in concert at Rye St Antony School (early February) www.oxfordmusicfestival.org | Entry: Check box office for ticket prices.

April to June

The Punt: Local bands at various city centre venues over two days (mid-May). | Entry: £5-£8 for weekend pass (some events are free).

July

Cornbury Music Festival: Big name acts play at Great Tew Estate near Banbury (early July). www.cornburyfestival.com | Entry: £200 for weekend, £79-£89 for day tickets.

Truck Festival: Big name acts and local musicians play at Hill Farm in Steventon (mid-July) www.truckfestival.com | Entry: £78

Riverside Festival: Local bands play at Charlbury near Oxford (late July). www.riversidefestival.charlbury.com | Entry: Free.

Global Gathering: Big name bands play at Long Marston Airfield in Straford Upon Avon (late July) www.globalgathering.com | Entry £88 for day tickets and £144 - £300 for weekend and VIP camping passes.

August
Wilderness Festival: Big name acts play at Cornbury Park in Charlbury over four days (early August).

www.wildernessfestival.com | Entry: £127-£152 for weekend tickets.

Fairport's Cropredy Convention: This legendary festival brings together the best of folk music over three days (early August). www.fairportconvention.com | Entry: £115 for weekend pass.

Reading Festival: Big name acts play at Rivermead Sports Centre in Reading over three days. www.readingfestival.com | Entry: £99 for day tickets and £213 for weekend pass.

October to December
OxJam Music Festival: Local bands across the UK perform to raise money for Oxfam (throughout October) www.oxfam.org.uk/oxjam | Entry: Varies but usually £8 per venue.

Oxford Chamber Music Festival: World-class classical musicians perform at Holywell Music Rooms, Oxford over three days. www.ocmf.net

Music Venues

O2 Academy on Cowley Road brings in big name bands and artists on a weekly basis, as well as regular club nights. It has two performance spaces (upstairs and downstairs), both of which have an intimate feel. A rare opportunity to see well-known acts up close and personal!
www.o2academyoxford.co.uk

There are several other venues where up-and-coming bands and artists perform. Here are a few worth checking out:

Jazz Night at the Art Bar If you are in the mood for some fun jazz, The Bullingdon Backroom on the Cowley Road is the place to spend your Tuesday evening. Every week they have a live jazz band in the back room of the bar, and it is usually packed with students. www.artbaroxford.co.uk

The Jericho Tavern on Walton Street is where Oxford-born bands Radiohead and Supergrass both performed in the early years. There is a regular Blues night on Mondays, and a range of other gigs throughout the year.
www.thejerichooxford.co.uk

Subverse at The Cellar is a niche house music radio show that airs throughout the week, founded by four Oxford students. They also host a fortnightly event at The Cellar in the city centre, providing new house, techno and bass music played by renowned DJs
www.facebook.com/SubverseRadio?fref=ts

Truck Music Store on Cowley Road is a music shop that sells loads of types of music in all kinds of formats. Additionally, they have frequent in-store shows with bands and artists playing various genres – everything from drum and bass to country and western, "with a fair few things in-between" according to their facebook page
www.truckmusicstore.co.uk | www.facebook.com/truckstoreoxford

The Wheatsheaf accessed via an alleyway on the High Street is a popular venue for local and visiting bands. Anything from acoustic singer songwriters to thrash metal. Crucially, their sound engineer is amazing. Check *The Nightshift* magazine for listings.
http://nightshift.oxfordmusic.net

Feeling Musical? Why not try an open mic night?

The Catweazle Club is the most popular open mic evening in Oxford. Held at the East Oxford Social Club, on the corner of Cowley Road and Princess Street, every Thursday at 8pm, Performers need to sign up by 7:30pm
http://catweazleclub.com | Entry £5/6 free for performers

Theatre

Oxford is a fantastic city for theatre. There are so many options in terms of venue, genre, amateur, professional, physical theatre to musicals, opera to modern dance. There is also a range of prices, and many theatres offer students discounted tickets.

New Theatre Oxford

The New Theatre, located on George Street was opened in 1934. This site is the main commercial theatre in Oxford, and has the capacity to hold 1,800 people. It is home to a wide range of shows from ballet and opera, to stand-up comedy and West End hits. It features two public bars as well as accessibility for people with reduced mobility, hearing and visual impairments. George Street, OX1 2AG | Tel: 0844 847 1585 | www.newtheatreoxford.org.uk

North Wall Arts Centre

The North Wall Arts Centre was completed in 2006 and has award-winning facilities such as studios, a public gallery and a theatre which seats 250 people. The theatre attracts up-and-coming acts, along with the well-known. South Parade, OX2 7NN | Tel: 01865 319450 | www.thenorthwall.com

Cornerstone Arts Centre

The Cornerstone Arts Centre offers many features to the public, such as a theatre auditorium holding shows and gigs, a bar and restaurant, a café, a visual art gallery and dance studios. The auditorium is fully air-conditioned and can hold **350 people standing and 224 people seated.** 25 Station Road, Didcot, Oxfordshire OX11 7NE | Tel: 01235 515144 | www.cornerstone-arts.org

Oxford Playhouse

The Oxford Playhouse was opened in 1938 and has a reputation for being one of Britain's leading theatres. It has had many famous people on its stage, including actors such as Dame Judi Dench, Dame Maggie Smith and Rowan Atkinson. The theatre seats 600 people, and holds an array of shows including poetry, contemporary dance and music, the best of British and international drama, student and amateur shows, family shows, comedy and lectures. 11-12 Beaumont Street, Oxford OX1 2LW | Tel: 01865 305305 | www.oxfordplayhouse.com

Old Fire Station

The Old Fire Station is an independent arts charity and has many facilities such as a theatre for music and drama, a gallery that holds exhibitions, a shop selling original artwork, workshops for artists and a studio for all kinds of dance. The theatre is partnered with the charity for the homeless, Crisis, and shares the building with Crisis Skylight Oxford. They train homeless and vulnerably housed people to help find and keep jobs through creative and formal learning. 40 George Street, Oxford, OX1 2AQ | Tel: 01865 263980 | www.oldfirestation.org.uk

Pegasus Theatre

The Pegasus Theatre was first opened in 1962 and was refurbished in 2010. The theatre holds music and drama productions from local and international companies, and professional dance performances. The main performance area is named after Philip Pullman, who is a major supporter and patron of the theatre. Magdalen Road, Oxford OX4 1RE. | Tel: 01865 812150 | www.pegasustheatre.org.uk

Oxford Theatre Guild

The Oxford Theatre Guild is an amateur theatre company that holds performances in many professional venues including the Oxford Playhouse. Although an amateur company, many former and current professionals are members. The Guild holds auditions for their productions, details of which can be found on their website. Trinity College Gardens (Parks Road entrance). | Tel: 01865 305305 | www.oxfordtheatreguild.com

The Theatre at Headington School

The theatre was built in 2002, and seats 240 people. The theatre has a licensed bar, and holds shows from leading touring companies as well as Headington School's own productions. The theatre plays a range of shows including dance, music, drama, lectures and comedy. Headington School, Oxford OX3 7TD | www.headington.org

Creation Theatre Company

The Creation Theatre Company has been around for 16 years. They specialise in site-specific inventive theatre in locations that have never been thought to be used for theatre. Their productions include fairy tales, classics, folk tales and Shakespeare, and are made to appeal to everyone. Tel: 01865 766266 | www.creationtheatre.co.uk

Oxford Shakespeare Company

The Oxford Shakespeare Company holds open-air, site-specific shows in the heart of Oxford and London during the summer. The company has been around since 2002, after taking over from the ten-year tenure of Bold & Saucy Theatre Company. It has an excellent reputation, and has been critically acclaimed for its interpretations of Shakespeare's plays and other classics. General Enquiries: 0844 879 4418 | www.osctheatre.org.uk | Bookings: 01865 305305 | www.ticketsoxford.com

For theatre listings, reviews, times, tickets and information go to www.inoxford.com/theatre/theatre_details

"The man who can drive himself further once the effort gets painful is the man who will win."

Roger Bannister, who ran the first sub-4-minute mile

on 6 May 1954 at Oxford University's Iffley Road Track.

SPORT & HEALTH

Oxford is a place teeming with people, be they newly arrived students, long-term professionals or part of the bustling tourist scene. It is a beautiful place to spend the day with a variety of attractions; a popular option is sport.

Gyms & Facilities

The town is filled with athletic opportunity, from sports clubs to raising money for a charity in the Oxford Half Marathon. Are you a keen athlete looking for training to take your career to the next level? Or do you just enjoy participating in sports? In the following pages you will see the variety of sporting options Oxford has to offer, with links to ever more wondrous events!

Oxford Brookes Sport There are two Brookes gyms: one is located alongside Cheney student village on Headington campus, the other is in Botley on Harcourt Hill campus. Don't think these gyms are exclusively for Brookes students – they are also open to the general public. Oxford Brookes students and staff do receive a higher discount but other Oxford students still get a good discounted deal.

> Brookes Sports Centre
>
> Headington Campus, Gipsy Ln, Oxford OX3 0BP
>
> Monday to Friday 7am to 11pm.
>
> Saturday to Sunday 9am to 10pm.
>
> Last entry to the gym is an hour before closing.
>
> www.brookes.ac.uk/brookes-sport/

The Centre holds a variety of equipment, including: a large range of free weights; resistance equipment; a climbing wall; squash courts; a basketball hall; and a health suite. For those looking for a general fitness area this is the perfect place.

As part of the health suite, you get access to the relaxing sauna and steam rooms to help after a stressful day of lectures or a particularly tough workout.

Also, the facility doesn't leave you drifting alone. If needed there are trained professionals and freelance personal trainers in-house to help you with any health, performance or fitness problems that may arise, be that paid-for sessions or a passing query about a certain exercise.

Alongside your own personal training the gym also offers a large range of classes. These include spinning, yoga, body combat, circuit training, break dance, zumba and many more.

Oxford University Sports Facilities Oxford University also has numerous sports grounds and facilities. Iffley Road hosts: a pool; a gym, a sports hall, an athletic track, astroturf and grass pitches, squash, tennis and badminton courts, and much more. Marston Road Sports Ground hosts regular football, cricket and rugby fixtures and accepts one-off bookings at set prices: cricket square (available April to July); rugby pitch (October to March); two football pitches (October to March); and changing facilities. The university parks are also available for hire. Oxford University offers Oxford students a higher discount, whilst still giving discounted rates to Oxford Brookes students.

LA Fitness This gym is one of 80 around the UK. As well as being part of a popular and reliable chain, LA Fitness Oxford contains a wide range of exercise equipment, training programmes, classes and leisure activities.

One of its key features is the quantity and quality of its gym machinery. The club is recognised for its impressive Technogym suite, where fitness specialists have brought together the best kit around to help improve all areas of your body. Alongside this is an extensive free weights room, cardio centre to work your heart and lungs, fixed strength machines and world-renowned Concept2 rowers used to help train Olympians.

As well as being a top-of-the-range fitness centre, LA Fitness Oxford provides swimming lessons for adults. You can take either single or group classes to help boost your confidence in the water. If you have children, there are also family-orientated activities and facilities for kids, such as swimming lessons from trained coaches who are part of the Amateur Swimming Association. If you would like to find out more go to:

> LA Fitness
> Monday to Thursday 6:30am to 10pm.
> Friday 6:30am to 8pm.
> Saturday and Sunday 9am to 5pm.
> Bank Holidays 9am to 5pm.

Oxford Ice Rink Not many cities in the UK have an ice rink but Oxford does! Located on Oxpens Road just a 10-minute walk from the city centre and railway station, Oxford Ice Rink offers facilities for ice hockey, figure skating, courses and even discos. For information about general opening hours and prices, visit the website at:
www.fusion-lifestyle.com/centres/Oxford_Ice_Rink

Events

Oxford Half Marathon

After its initial start in 2011 the Oxford Half Marathon has grown year-on-year in both number of contestants and money raised. The 13-mile run is in aid of local Oxford charities.

The event is becoming more popular each year and takes an incredible amount of preparation and cooperation. It is all made possible by a large number of people and organisations that invest time and money into making the run both safe and enjoyable. Some of the core groups behind this are the Oxford City Council, Oxfordshire emergency services and Oxfordshire City Council, who are vital in the planning of the event. Each year a number of sponsors, varying from Lidl to Up and Running, help the day run smoothly and with as little trouble as possible.

Like all races there is also an element of competitiveness to the day. Each contestant will get a medal and T-shirt while a select few also get the chance to win a mystery prize for coming first in a selection of different categories, varying with age, gender and group quantity.

While the event is open to a limited number of runners, there is no limit to the help needed during the run. Volunteers are always desired for a variety of tasks, so if you are unable to run you can still make a difference. More details can be found online at:

www.oxfordhalf.co.uk

Ping!Oxford

At numerous places around Oxford you will find a table tennis table with bat and ball, on which you can play for free! Ping!Oxford is part of a national incentive, started during the run-up to the 2012 Olympics, encouraging people to go outdoors, play table tennis, and have fun. This has spiralled into key community hotspots for a casual bit of sport and 500 tables all around the UK.

Yet the fun doesn't stop there; after playing numerous games with your friends you can enter tournaments organised at various sites in which you can compete whilst having a relaxing day out. Throughout the summer the tables will host friendly competitions to keep the excitement and fervour alive.

The initiative continues further by offering detailed links to local table tennis clubs and contests in order to support people in getting involved in their passion. So why not pick up a paddle and give it a go? It's fun, free and you may find a new and healthy hobby to fill those lazy afternoons.

For more details about table locations, events and connections go to:

www.pingoxford.co.uk/index.php

Headington Festival and Sports Day

The Headington Festival and Sports Day is a fun-filled afternoon, usually held on the first Sunday in June, where families and locals come for hours of action-packed excitement.

The festival began in 2003 and has since been a continuing success, hosting up to 3,000 people each time. In conjunction with Oxford City Council, the charity Headington Action brings together neighbourhood services and produce providers to create an aura of community spirit. The festival holds around 60 stalls containing a mixture of local farmers and entertainment vendors, all looking to help improve awareness of local produce.

Let us not forget the sport element of this day, with a key part of the afternoon being a mixture of fantastic childhood activities including: welly wanging, face painting, dress-up contests, and other outdoor games. The day is also supported by nearby sport clubs and organisations in order to promote activity in the local area.

For further information about the yearly Headington Festival and Sports Day please look online at:
www.headingtonfestival.co.uk

The Boat Race

Since 1856 the Boat Race has been held annually between the Oxford University Boat Club and the Cambridge University Boat Club. The event usually takes place on the last weekend of March or start of April, on the River Thames in London. The race starts at Putney Bridge and finishes at Chiswick Bridge, so go along to see the Oxford team in action!
www.theboatrace.org

Health

Emergency Services - regardless of your nationality, there is no charge for calling an ambulance or receiving accident & emergency (A&E) treatment in the UK.

> Call 999 if you require an ambulance or urgent medical assistance
>
> Call 111 if you need medical help fast, but it isn't an emergency.

Long term residents - if you are an international student studying full-time in the UK for more than six months, you are entitled to free healthcare during your period of study.

Short term residents - if you are studying part-time, or for less than six months, you *may* be entitled to free healthcare during your stay. Check the UKCISA website for more details www.ukcisa.org.uk/International-Students/Study-work--more/Health-and-healthcare/

Documentation - whatever your study situation, if you are from outside the UK you will need to provide evidence of your entitlement to free healthcare in the form of passport, visa, or letters from your place of study.

Prescriptions - If you take regular medication it is a good idea to bring with you copies of your prescriptions and a letter from your doctor, to avoid delays in dispensing.

Hospitals

The John Radcliffe Hospital (known as "the JR") is Oxford's main hospital for accidents and emergencies (A&E) and is open 24 hours a day. It is located in Headington, approximately three miles east of the Oxford city centre. It is a short bus ride from the centre. The JR also has a children´s emergency department, which is open from 10am until 8pm.

Horton General Hospital, located in Banbury, also offers 24-hour A&E treatment. It is a little over an hour from the city centre by public transportation.

There are a number of other hospitals offering specialist medical treatment and advice .

Churchill Hospital: 01865 741841
Old Road, Oxford, OX3 7LE

Horton General Hospital: 01295 275500
Oxford Road, Banbury, OX16 9AL

John Radcliffe Hospital: 01865 741166
Headley Way, Oxford, OX3 9DU

Nuffield Orthopaedic Centre: 01865 741155
Windmill Road, Oxford, OX3 7LD

The Manor Hospital: 0800 015 5020
Beech Road, Oxford, OX3 7RP

Warneford Hospital: 01865 741717
Warneford Lane, Oxford, OX3 7JX

Health Centres

For those of you who are moving to Oxford, it is advisable to register with your local health centre. This is your first point of contact for for medical advice and prescriptions. You are usually expected to schedule an appointment to see a doctor (GP) or nurse, although some do offer drop-in sessions.

Bury Knowles Health Centre: 01865 308400
207 London Road, Headington, OX3 9JA

Donnington Health Centre: 01865 771207
1 Henley Avenue, Oxford, OX4 4DH

Jericho Health Centre: 01865 311234
Walton Street, Oxford, OX2 6NW

St Bartholomew's Medical Centre 01865 242334
Manzil Way, Cowley Road, Oxford, OX4 1XB

Summertown Health Centre: 01865 515552
160 Banbury Road, Oxford, OX2 7BS

Oxford Brookes Medical Centre

For Brookes students, the Oxford Brookes Medical Centre offers a variety of services and information. Based on the Headington Hill campus, services range from medical advice and contraception to help with eating disorders.

Outside surgery hours or in vacation periods you can also go to St Bartholomew's Medical Centre.

Dentist

If you are looking for a caring, professional and experienced dentist that is based in a convenient location then head straight for the Oxford Dental Centre. It is situated in the heart of Oxford, just a short walk from the town centre up Banbury Road in Summertown. It is a long-running practice renowned for its quality care.

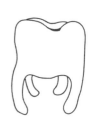

Oxford Dental Centre
162 Banbury Road, Oxford, OX2 7BT
Monday to Friday 8am to 5pm
Thursday till 7pm

Call 01865 515 806 for appointments
or 07985 716665 for an emergency
www.oxforddentalcentre.co.uk

Alternatively, you could visit the Studental clinic based within the Oxford Brookes Headington Hill Campus. Studental is not a student-specific practice, it is open to everyone. Booking an appointment online couldn't be easier, with a range of times and dates are available – you can even choose which dentist you want within the practice.

Studental
Oxford Brookes University,
Headington, OX4 0BP
Monday to Thursday 8am to 6:30pm
Friday 8am to 6pm

Call 01865 484608 for appointments
www.studental.co.uk

"The SU plays an important role, supporting the serious academic issues as well as the fun, extracurricular stuff too."

Cara Gresly,

Students' Union Representative

STUDENTS' UNION

What is the Students' Union?

The Students' Union was originally founded in 1922, and after the First World War and is constituted under the 1994 Education Act. There are 600 Students' Unions in the UK, collectively managed by the National Union of Students (NUS). The ultimate purpose of Students' Unions is to democratically represent the interests of their members, but Students' Unions do much more than just political wrangling; they ensure every element of your university life is perfect for you. Each Students' Union (SU) is responsible for the creation of different clubs and societies, such as, but not restricted to: politics societies, sports societies, and art societies. You can find a huge number of societies which can cover many different interests. If you can't find a society you're interested in, get in touch with your SU and start your own!

The SU is a separate body from the university, here to represent you and help you get the most out of your time studying. The SU plays an important role, lobbying the serious academic issues as well as supporting the fun extracurricular stuff. Students' Unions are present in all the universities of England, and Oxford is no exception. We have Oxford Students' Union, and Oxford Brookes Students' Union; each of them is adapted to their university, and their respective student populations.

What can the SU do for you?

Practical things the SU can help you with:

- Securing accommodation and checking tenancy agreements.

- Advising you on your student rights, academic issues and student finance.

- Connecting you with clubs and societies.

- Give general advice and support on coping with student life.

Student Discounts

There are too many concessions and special discounts given to students to list them all here, but most high-street retailers offer discounts to students.

To make sure you are making the most of your student status, don't forget to buy an NUS card - you can apply online at cards.nusextra.co.uk/. This will give you access to many exclusive student discounts!

Because there is more to life than just studying, here are our top five ideas for extracurricular pursuits

1. Raise money for charity

2. Start a club

3. Join a band

4. Host dinner parties

5. Start a business

"Life is like riding a bicycle. To keep your balance you must keep moving."

Albert Einstein

TRANSPORT

Getting to Oxford

By Plane

While Oxford has an airport of its own at Kidlington, it is used mainly for private and charter aircraft and has very few scheduled domestic or international flights. The nearest commercial airports to Oxford are those around London, to the south-east, or Birmingham, to the north. Most foreign travellers prefer the London based airports Heathrow and Gatwick. Heathrow is the closer of the two to Oxford, and road access from both Heathrow and Gatwick is via the M25 (heading north and west respectively).

The Oxford Bus Company runs several airport bus services from the central Gloucester Green bus station (the coach stops along the High Street, outside Oxford Brookes University and in Headington, as well as other stops once the bus has left Oxford).

The Heathrow Express runs every half an hour from 4am to 10pm and hourly from midnight to 4am (Cost - £19 approx. Duration - 70 minutes)

The Gatwick Express runs hourly from 5.15am to 8.15pm and every two hours from 10pm to 4am. (Cost - £27. Duration - 2 hours)

The National Express Bus Company also runs less frequent airport bus services to Luton Airport and to Stansted Airport. For these airports it is best to check the websites and Gloucester Green timetables.

Birmingham Airport is smaller and has fewer destinations than the London airports, but it is definitely the closest to Oxford in terms of public transport travel time. Birmingham International Airport has its own railway station, which is connected to the airport terminal building via the free AirRail Link shuttle. From the railway station, trains depart to and from Oxford every hour between 06:14 and 22:14 and take about an hour. A single ticket costs £25.50, a return £28.80 off-peak or £51 at peak travel times. You can get discounted tickets by booking in advance or by investing in a Young Persons Railcard. Check timetables and rail websites prior to travelling.

By Road
Oxford is linked to London by the south-eastern stretch of the M40 motorway (depending on traffic, which can be heavy, the journey varies between 50-90 min). The north-western continuation of the M40 also links Oxford with Birmingham, and the West Midlands.

Parking and access restrictions are very stringent in the narrow streets of central Oxford. The roads are under constant surveillance by wardens and cameras and there is a risk of heavy fines. The council has also implemented circuitous and one-way traffic systems, making it difficult to get around by car. However, visitors driving to Oxford from the south have easy access to the Westgate multi-story car park on Oxpens Road.

An alternative is to use one of the five Park and Ride services which are located in the city outskirts on all sides of Oxford (well signposted). They offer free, or cheap, parking and, once on the Park and Ride bus, are about 12 minutes from city centre. £2 is charged for the return bus trip to the city centre. Be wary of using the Thornhill Park and Ride on weekdays, as it is very busy early on due to the London commuters.

By Train
The Oxford railway station is in the western part of the city centre. Fast First Great Western run trains to and from London Paddington every half an hour, taking about an hour to complete the journey. Commonly, these trains call at Reading, Slough (for Windsor Castle), and Didcot Parkway, though not all trains call at each of these stations. Tickets to London cost approximately £20 off-peak without a railcard and £40 at peak times without a railcard, although you can buy tickets from about £4 if you book in advance and online. There are also stopping services to London calling at a large number of stations, which run every hour and take about 90 minutes to complete the journey.

Other Destinations
First Great Western also runs hourly trains on the Cotswold line to Worcester and also to Bicester.

Cross Country Trains also run through Oxford, mostly running to/from Manchester and Southampton. These trains run half-hourly in both directions but stop at about 9pm. All of these trains stop at Reading going south, and Leamington Spa for Warwick and Warwick Castle, and Birmingham going north.

Most trains into Oxford allow bicycles to be carried for free. But you may need to book, and it can depend on space being available.

By Bus

Frequent services run from several convenient bus stops to Gloucester Green coach station in Oxford. Those coming from London (called the Oxford Tube) begin at Victoria Station, running westwards via Marble Arch, Notting Hill and Shepherd's Bush and then on to Oxford. Stops in Oxford include, beside others, Thornhill Park and Ride, Headington, Brookes University, St Clement's, High Street (Queen's Lane),(which is best for daily visitors, as it's right in the middle of the city centre), and finally, Gloucester Green, which is also well situated. Bus companies between London and Oxford include all of those mentioned before.

There are regular bus services between Oxford and London's Heathrow and Gatwick airports with the 'airline'. bus.

There is also an X5 bus between Oxford and Cambridge, taking approximately 3 hours and 20 minutes, as well as buses from Bicester and Banbury operated by Stagecoach. There are also several coaches from other parts of the country that are run by National Express.

Getting Around Oxford

On Foot

Oxford city centre is very compact and easy to walk around. Many areas of the city centre are pedestrianised, and all major tourist sites are well signposted.

All the streets of the city centre, including the small and narrow, are pedestrian friendly but difficult for cars.

The best thing to do when walking around on foot is to use a map, we've included the key areas in this guide, however more detailed maps are available in any newsagent as well as WHSmith and the Tourist Information Centre on Broad Street or online if you have a smartphone.

By Bicycle

Many students use bicycles to get around and, as in Amsterdam or Copenhagen, there are thousands of them. Although there are cycle lanes on virtually every street near the centre, they do share the road with other motorists. Extra care should be taken cyling around buses which have blindspots where cyclists cannot be seen. Never cycle past on the inside of buses or lorries.

The familiar sight of cyclists to local drivers makes cycling safer than in other towns, but many accidents happen each year, often due to dangerous cycling. If you are thinking of cycling in the UK, make sure you are familliar with the UK Highway Code for cyclists as laws do apply. It is also vital that you use lights at night; local police frequently set up checkpoints and there is a fine for cycling without lights.

Bike parking is available everywhere, just be sure to buy a strong lock to keep it safe, and don't leave anything valuable on the bike.

The best information can be found on the Cycle into Oxford map, available from the tourist office (15 Broad Street Oxford, OX1 3AS), which shows all local cycle routes. You can also hire bikes from Cyclo Analysts (150 Cowley Rd; £10/27 per day/week).

Buying a Bicycle

A lot of people choose to invest in a bicycle. They're tremendously useful in Oxford: quick, reliable (or at least, with bike shops all over Oxford, never too difficult to fix), and a good sort of on-the-go exercise for busy types. Something worth remembering though: bike thieves are everywhere, and tend to have lots of free time on their hands - so get a decent lock, and don't use your £600 racing/road bike to get to lectures. It is worth buying a cheaper, second-hand one for £30 or so for day-to-day travel.

By Car

It is best to avoid driving in central Oxford. Traffic is heavy, the one-way system can be complicated to newcomers, the streets are often very narrow, with restrictions, and parking can be expensive. It is advised to use public transport such as the Park and Ride bus system where possible.

Commuting

The weekday traffic tends to build up between 7.15am to 9.30am and 3.30pm to 6.45pm. The city centre and areas around the hospitals are generally the first areas to become congested and if possible should be avoided to ease travel. When entering Oxford from the North, Kidlington and the Pear Tree interchange are usually when you will approach most of the traffic.

Allow extra time for bus and car journeys during peak traffic, and we recommend adding an extra 30 minutes to get around during rush hour.

Parking In and Around the City

Westgate Car Park: Average 2 Stars in reviews: Sunday-Friday £2.50 per hour.

Worcester Street Car Park: Average 2 Stars in reviews: Sunday - Friday £3.30 per hour.

A popular parking website to look at before travelling is: www.parkatmyhouse.com and search for Oxford. This allows students or commuters to arrange low-cost parking with residents. You can pay to park on their driveway, certifying your parking space for as long as you need.

Park and Ride

The Park and Rides are a popular choice amongst commuters and visitors to Oxford. On average they offer cheaper parking than directly in the centre, and regular buses provide good value and flexibility.

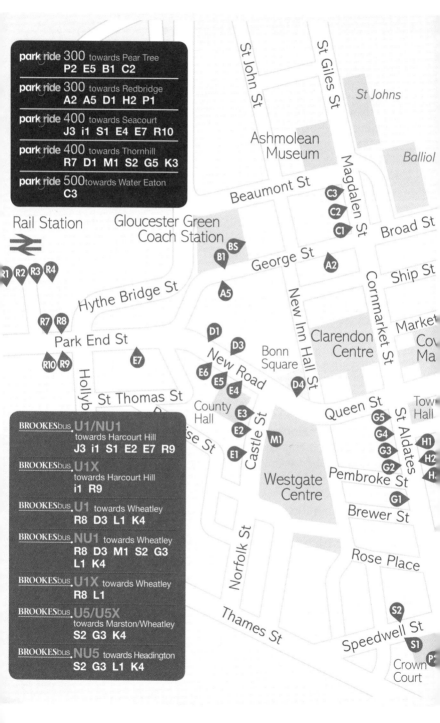

Where to catch your bus in Oxford City Centre

correct at September 2014

Parks Rd

Trinity

Holywell St

Sheldonian Theatre

Bodleian Library

All Souls

Radcliffe Camera

Queens

K1 **K2** **K3** **K4** **K5**

High St

L1

J3 **J2** **J1**

i1

Merton St

Corpus Christi

Merton

ristchurch

Cathedral

P1 Police Station

C1 Bus Stops
not to scale

city 2 towards Kidlington	**C1**
city 3 towards Rose Hill	**R1 R7 D1 D4 K2**
city 3 towards Rail Station	**J3 i2 S1 E6 E7 R10**
city 4 towards Wood Farm	**R7 D1 M1 S2 G1 K3**
city 4 towards Botley	**J3 i1 S1 E2 E7 R10**
city 5 towards Blackbird Leys	**R2 R7 D1 M1 S2 G4 K1**
city 5 towards Rail Station	**J3 i2 S1 E6 E7**
city 6 towards Wolvercote	**C3**
city 8/9 towards Barton/Risinghurst	**E3 K4**
city 13 towards JR Hospital	**R4 R7 D1 M1 S2 G2 K3**
city X13 towards JR Hospital	**P2 G2 K3**
city 13 towards Rail Station	**J3 i2 S1 E6 E7**
city X3 towards Rail Station	**P2 E6 E7**
city X3 towards Abingdon	**R3 R7 D1 H1 P1**
city X13 towards Abingdon	**J3 i2 H1 P1**
city 35 towards Kennington	**H3 P1**

airline **LHR** towards Heathrow Airport	**BS** Bay7 **S2 K5**
airline **LGW** towards Gatwick Airport	**BS** Bay6 **S2 K5**

X90 towards London Victoria	**BS** Bay5 **S2 K5**

By Bus

Local buses are mostly operated by the Oxford Bus Company and Stagecoach. Fares are expensive (but less so than in other British cities) and a flat single rate within the city was recently introduced. If you plan on making more than two trips in a day, it might be worth buying an all-day pass to save money. The main hubs for local buses are the rail station, St Giles and St Aldate's. If you are in town for a while, you may want a rechargeable smart-card that gives discounts on bus fares. With a BROOKESKEY pricing is discounted quite heavily in the city and reasonably well on trips to other major cities.

The BROOKESKEY also allows free travel on all the Brookes Bus services and is very handy for travelling around the city. The service covers a large area from Gipsy Lane, to Wheatley, Harcourt Hill, and Cowley. (U1 / U1X / U5 / U5X)

Travel Shops

The Oxford Bus Company has two Travel Shops in Oxford. Here you can receive information on bus times, ticket prices, and top up your bus card. These information centres are located on the High Street and on the 3rd floor of Debenhams on Magdalen St.

> ### The Debenhams Travel Shop
> ### Opening hours
> Monday to Wednesday 9:30am to 6pm
> Thursday 9:30am to 8pm
> Friday 9:30am to 6pm
> Saturday 9am to 6pm
> Sunday 11am to 5pm

By Taxi

Oxford has both black cabs (also known as Hackney Carriages), which can be flagged down from the street or taken from taxi stands located around the city, and 'minicabs' which must be ordered by phone. Meter taxis are quite pricey but are convenient

for short hops if travelling in a big group. Minicabs are much cheaper for long-distance journeys - the fare should be agreed over the phone when booking or should be bargained with the driver - never get in a minicab without agreeing the price or checking they have a hackney carriage licence. Some local firms offer both hire cars and taxi cabs.

Taxis: There are taxi ranks at the train station and bus station, as well as on St Giles and at Carfax. Be prepared to join a long queue after closing time.

Tip Beat the late-night queues and save some money by walking in to the minicab HQ on St Aldate's.

Safety Alert!

If you are hailing a black cab

• Check that proper licence plates are displayed on the front or rear of the vehicle.
• Check the meter is set to the minium fare as you get in.
• Always sit in the back of the vehicle.

If you have booked a private hire taxi

• Confirm that the driver knows your name, destination, and the licence plate matches the one given on booking.
• Check before getting in how much the fare will be and ensure you have the amount ready.

Always check the driver is displaying a valid ID badge

Need a Cab?

001 Taxis: **01865 240000**

A2B Oxford Taxi: **01865 477777 / 01865 477477**

ABC Taxis: **01865 770077 / 01865 775577**

Elite Cars: **01865 250500**

Oxford Cars: **01865 406070 / 01865 406080**

Oxford City Cars: **01865 703030 / 01865 703333**

Radio Taxis: **01865 242424 / 01865 249743**

Royal Cars: **01865 777333**

Star Cars: **01865 777695**

Day Trips and National Travel

Getting to London by Bus

One of the great things about living in Oxford is its proximity to London. The Oxford–London bus route is busy, with three companies offering services throughout the day and night. Most, if not all, services are reliable and all start their journey at Gloucester Green bus station, going up through Headington, stopping at Brookes and the Thornhill Park and Ride. In the UK, it is customary to pay the bus driver as you get on the bus. Make sure you have money in your wallet as they usually only accept cash or prepaid travel cards.

Oxford Tube Runs every 10 minutes to Buckingham Palace Rd (return £13, 1½ hours). www.oxfordtube.com

X90 Oxford Express Runs up to every 15 minutes to Victoria Coach Station (Cost - Return £13 approx. Duration - 1½ hours). www.oxfordbus.co.uk

Megabus Coaches run every half an hour to Buckingham Palace Road (Cost - One way from £1. Duration - 1¼ hours).
www.megabus.com

Getting to London and elsewhere by Train

There are half-hourly services to London Paddington (£18.80, one hour); and approximately every hour to Birmingham (£20, 1¼ hours), Worcester (£16.40, 1½ hours) and Hereford (£14.70, two hours). Hourly services also run to Bath (£17.20, 1¼ hours) and Bristol (£18.70, 1½ hours) but require a change at Didcot Parkway.

More Bus Routes

National Express has five direct buses to Birmingham (Cost - £10.20. Duration - 2 hours). One service to Bath (Cost - £8.90. Duration - 2 hours) and Bristol (Cost - £12. Duration - 2 /4 hours). Again, these services start their journey at Gloucester Green bus station.

Stagecoach serves most of the small towns in Oxfordshire and runs the X5 service to Cambridge (£7, 3½ hours) roughly every half-hour. If you're planning a lot of bus journeys it's worth buying a Goldrider pass (£18), which allows unlimited bus travel in Oxfordshire for seven days.

Accessible Oxford Transport

Motability

This is a scheme to provide for the purchase or lease of vehicles to people on mobility allowance.

Tel: 0845 456 4566
Minicom: 0845 6750009
Disabled Motoring UK

This is the campaigning charity for disabled motorists, passengers and Blue Badge holders.
Tel: 01598 489449
www.disabledmotoring.org
email: info@disabledmotoring.org

Transport Direct

This is a service where you can plan a journey door-to-door.
www.transportdirect.info

Wheelchair accessible Taxis

001 Taxis: 01865 240000
A1 Taxis: 01865 248000
Radio Taxis: 01865 242424

Bus Services - City and Local

The County Council operates a Concessionary Fares scheme which gives benefits for buses for residents with disabilities. Leaflets and application forms are available from Oxford City Council, St Aldate's Chambers, 109 St Aldate's, Oxford OX1 1DS, Tel 01865 252646.

Permit for Travel for Mobility Scooters

All users of mobility scooters must obtain prior approval of operators and obtain a standard 'permit for travel' prior to travelling on a bus with their scooter. This can be obtained from Stagecoach Oxfordshire and can be used on all the local buses.
Tel: 01865 772250
Email: oxford.enquiries@stagecoachbus.com

Car Access to Bus Station

Cars are not normally permitted into the bus station, so you need to make arrangements in advance if you wish to be dropped off or collected. 24 hours' notice is recommended.
Tel 01865 794307.

Railway Station

The Railway Station has an accessible WC and lifts. Buses, most of which are accessible, stop immediately outside, and there is also a Taxi rank immediately outside, all approached via gentle ramps.

Passengers with disabilities should pre-arrange their journey to ensure that the necessary support is available to them and details can be obtained from a leaflet in the railway station for disabled passengers which also contains an application form for the disabled persons' Railcard.

For deaf and hearing-impaired travellers a National Rail Enquiries minicom service is based in Reading on 0845 6050600.

Park and Ride

All Park & Ride buses have the wheelchair accessible 'kneeling step' with fold-down ramp.

Parking

On-street parking will require a Blue Badge in the relevant parking bays. There are 90 disabled parking bays throughout the city. Again, a Blue Badge must be displayed showing its number.

For further information telephone Oxfordshire Social Services on: 0845 0507 666.

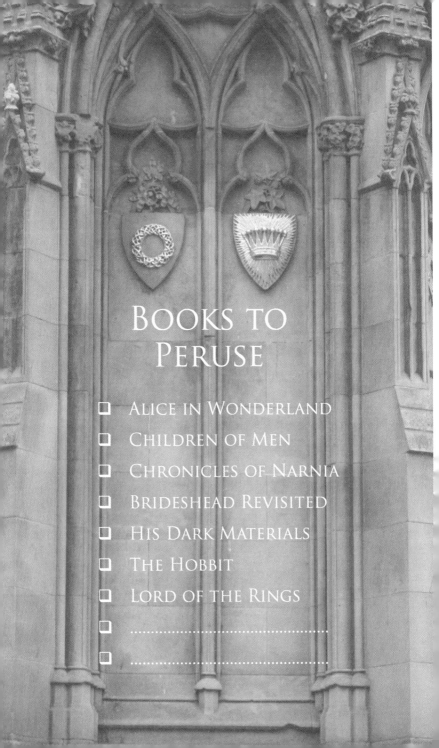

Books to Peruse

- ☐ Alice in Wonderland
- ☐ Children of Men
- ☐ Chronicles of Narnia
- ☐ Brideshead Revisited
- ☐ His Dark Materials
- ☐ The Hobbit
- ☐ Lord of the Rings
- ☐ ....
- ☐ ....

PLACES TO SEE

1. _____ ☐

2. _____ ☐

3. _____ ☐

4. _____ ☐

5. _____ ☐

6. _____ ☐

7. _____ ☐

8. _____ ☐

9. _____ ☐

10. _____ ☐

PHOTOS TO TAKE

1. ☐

2. ☐

3. ☐

4. ☐

5. ☐

6. ☐

7. ☐

8. ☐

9. ☐

10. ☐

Meet the team

Graphic Design & Production

Copy Editor & Marketing

Copy Editor

Chapter Editor

Chapter Editor &
Marketing

Chapter Editor

Graphic Design &
Production

Chapter Editor

Production &
Finance